Reflections on Christmas

Reflections on Christmas

— Seasonal poems —
by Chris Leonard and Eric Leat

CWR

Published 2013 by CWR, Waverley Abbey House, Waverley Lane, Farnham,
Surrey GU9 8EP, UK. CWR is a Registered Charity – Number 294387 and a
Limited Company registered in England – Registration Number 1990308.

For list of National Distributors visit www.cwr.org.uk/distributors

Concept development, editing, design and production by CWR
Printed in the UK by Page Brothers

ISBN: 978-1-85345-999-3

Contents

Introduction

Not long after my first book was published, I decided that now I was 'A Writer', I had better write verses to go with my Christmas cards: just simple ones, to give pleasure or maybe make people stop and think for a moment. Putting these together with other seasonal poems over two decades later, I wondered if they would make a book. After all, poetry has a special place at Christmas time, with new material sought for reading aloud in services, concerts, gatherings of all kinds ... and to aid quiet reflection amidst the rush.

Then I thought of how much I and others love Eric's poems, some of which I compiled into a self-published booklet for him in 2008. They work so well when read out loud – some are funny, but all have a depth and simplicity which comes from the life-long faith of someone nearing 90. Although a generation apart in age, Eric and I share a love of poetry, we have both had some poems published, we are members of the same church and we both live in a road called after a famous poet in the appropriately-named village of Bookham, Surrey.

Some of our poems focus on thankfulness, celebration and wonder, others on those 'hanging from edges'. Eric and I hope you'll find plenty to reflect on and enjoy in this book, reading perhaps a poem or two at a time, during this special season.

Chris Leonard
Bookham, Surrey

Preparing for Christmas

The Cross in the Star

I know it's all been said before
on countless Christmas cards in rhyme,
but still it should be said again
that love came down at Christmas time.

And so I pray that you may know
through all the parties and the fun
that Christ the Lord is still with us
the gift of God, His only Son.

So come with me to Bethlehem
where worldly wealth is turned to dross
and find the pearl of greatest price
for in His star you'll see the cross.

Highly Favoured Lady

There can be no resurrection
without a death.
No death without a life,
no life without a birth,
no birth without a conception.

So we praise You, mighty God,
for Mary, highly favoured,
for her glad acceptance
of the word of Your angel, Gabriel,
and the joy inside her.
For her words of praise
rejoicing in God her Saviour.

All generations call her 'Blessed'.

Maternity Ward

I had my first baby just before Christmas,
in a hospital, neat and orderly.
All night long, the nurses raved at a party
in their home across the car park.
I laboured, staring at a sheet of paper
with a coach and four
someone had stuck upon the door.

The next night, nurses came round
with lanterns, singing carols.
'Away in a manger', they sang,
as I lay on the hospital bed, cradling my new son.
They'd wound red ribbon round the handle of a crib,
ready for a Christmas baby, but none came.
'How awful, being in hospital over Christmas!'
   people said,
but I thought the time appropriate to have a baby
and the place much safer than a stable!

Bethlehem

Hannah, our midwife in the village,
said it won't be long now –
perhaps a week or two.
Then, of all times, Joseph said:
'We have to go to Bethlehem.'
Why Bethlehem?

'Sorry love; the Romans say
we have to go to where we come from
to be registered.
You know what they're like.'
So; Bethlehem!

Joseph has bought a donkey
to carry me and our things.
He's strong, says he will walk.
But ... Bethlehem!

I reckon it will be soon,
calculating from when the angel
came to me that night,
and came to Joseph too, dear Joseph.
It's a long way, Bethlehem.

Few people have heard of Bethlehem
where my child, the Son of God, Jesus,
will be born.
The city of David,
yes; Bethlehem.

Always Room for Angels

If I had been God
I'd have arranged it all
quite differently;
after all, my only son.
His birth would have been
altogether grander,
more fitting.
Comfort and cleanliness
would have been my watchwords.

God knows best, I guess,
but how odd to choose
a stable!
Surrounded by beasts,
grubby shepherds to visit,
not enough room to swing a cat.
And yet room enough
for the heavenly hosts
to find their way in.
But then think how many angels
you can get on the head of a pin.

The Christmas Star

The Christmas star of all the stars tonight
shines bright – so bright
that on their knees the shepherds fall,
their eyes on fire, their hearts appalled,
until the words the angels sing –
'PEACE ... A SAVIOUR ... COME ...'

The Christmas lights in High Streets tinsel-hung
flash on and off and off and on,
and TV shows from every window blaze –
carols, East Enders, magic to amaze.
Images splinter. Amid the jarring din
we lose the words the angels sing.
'PEACE ... A SAVIOUR ... COME ...'

PEACE, in all the Christmas whirl
of cards to write and plans unfurled.
A SAVIOUR, as the tension builds,
from squabbles, greed, hopes unfulfilled.
COME, fix your eyes on that bright star.
He has drawn near Who was afar.

No Room

There was no room for God
in the busy bustling inn,
customers calling for food and drink,
shouting their orders above the din.
Bedrooms all booked and tables filled.
Merchants with profits, soldiers with pay,
the innkeeper beaming as the money rolled in;
who wants a poor man and wife in the family way?
Well; there is the old stable, it's only a shack,
you'll find it up the path there, round the back.

I believe in God all right,
you know, I pray and that
when I need to, when money's tight
or things go wrong. But there's so much rat
racing. My boss wants everything
done yesterday. Now it's Christmas once more:
turkey, presents, hang up your stocking.
Stocking? Pillow case, half the lounge floor ...
Must have a few jars with the lads in the pub.
Expect me to go to church? Give it a miss,
no room for that God stuff at a time like this.

We are unclean and cannot worship with the others.
No one wants us in their home,
we are shepherds, caring for the sheep,
busy through the night when the lambs come.
But it was to us the angels spoke.
'A Saviour is born unto you,' they cried.
We went to the stable and no one said:
'You cannot go in, you are not clean, stay outside.'
Yes, we were there, and found we were able
to kneel and to worship God in a stable.

Christmas Confusion

In July as I buy suntan lotion and maps
our letterbox drops, with a flip and a flap.
A warm fireside scene in red, gold and green,
the first Christmas catalogue (pause while I scream!)

September the first, I go looking for eggs
(not for Easter – the sort chickens lay),
but I find Christmas puddings, mince pies,
    Christmas cakes,
a thumping great Yuletide display.

November the second, I want to buy ham
and perhaps a samosa or two,
but right 'cross the deli, in script red as jelly,
it says, 'MERRY CHRISTMAS TO YOU'
and I think to myself that this stuff will not last
in the fridge until then – I'm confused!

December the tenth and I'm on a quest,
teenage son has a birthday that's due.
I reject cards of Santa, and sleigh bells, and deer,
he'd prefer a Ferrari or bottle of beer,
but he's not going to get one, at least till next year
and cute angels just simply won't do!

As December progresses, it's Scrooge who impresses
and I'm lacking in seasonal cheer,
for by day number eighteen dread Sales are awaiting
and Easter begins the New Year.

By Two-O-One-Eight I hope to migrate
for a barbeque Christmas in sun,
shut myself in a crate, or else hibernate
but I hope that your Christmas is fun!

Refuged or Refugee?

Cosy and warm,
safe from all harm;
family there,
not one with a care.
Presents and booze,
a post-dinner snooze,
no work to do
till the holiday's through –
and perhaps the new year
will bring some more cheer
to those who don't muse
too much on the news.

So far from home
as birth-pangs make groan,
the young girl feels fear
and a sheep nudges near.
'Oh God, where are you?'
Sobs, 'What are we to do?'
Once born, scant respite,
they must flee in the night.
And all that they hope
for our world and their land
is held in the grasp
of a tiny frail hand.

Outside or Inside

Room for the soldiers,
the strong and the healthy,
room for the taxman,
the harlots, the wealthy;
but no room for Mary,
no room for the birth
of the King of kings
coming to visit the Earth.

The ox and the sheep,
the goats and the pigeons
will all be received
in the Temple of God
for the sacrifice.

But the Lord Himself
will be sacrificed
outside the Temple,
outside the city.
Sacrificed for us
that we may no longer
be outside, but made welcome, inside.

Anno Domini

Across the nation, a thousand
'Marys', aged five,
innocent of baby bumps,
tea towels slipping,
act out scenes set shortly before,
and after, an un-sterile birth.
Quite unaccountably,
we hope again for the world.

A lorry driver spends his Christmas
discovering where joy meets sorrow
in foreign war zone.
He causes children's faces
to light up.
We see it on TV.

Messiah shakes cathedral vaulting,
thrills the ear's drum, bones and spaces,
twitches the corner of
some holy place's curtain.
We glimpse dimensions beyond
musical virtuosity.
At the darkest time of year
once, a birth floodlit worlds
for shepherds and kings –
changed everything.
Anno Domini.

Suns burnt supernova
when God fused with man.
Flashes of that brilliance reach through, despite
all that we have done to 'Xmas',
and cause our tired eyes
to melt with tears.

Winter Morning

Dulled, in December
I stare through double glass
at drops which shimmer
like diamonds in dankness.
They catch the little light,
dance with it
and fall.

Another swells, globing brightness
for a second, for a hopeful minute
before the wind
flicks it off the bare twig
onto the sodden grass beneath.

Why do I slump at the dark year's ebb
despite all beauty
despite knowing that this morning
I should be energising
Christmas?

Celebrating Christmas

Unto You is Born

Not unto peoples nor nations
not to the vast generations
not to the Gentile nor the Jew
no, but unto you, unto you
the Saviour who is Christ, is born.

For unto you is born this One
who is the Word made flesh, God's Son,
to no one else in your life, none
but you. For you alone is come
the Saviour who is Christ the Lord.

First published in The Christian, 1996

A Happy Christmas!

High notes hang in the frosty air.
There's mince pies and warm spiced wine,
and glints of red and green and gold.
Then cards arrive, I hear
from friends I haven't seen all year.
Generations gather to enjoy
times familiar and yet new,
silly games and laughing till it hurts.
Best is relaxing afterwards with friends
with time expanding after all the rush –
and those moments when something fresh
springs from the old story,
and the Christ-child
brushes my cheek with His finger.
Tradition and surprise
wrap up Christmas.

Christmas Present

A cliché in red and gold packaging,
illusion of rich cosiness, unpeeled
reveals the object
of a desire, designed to satisfy –
for ten minutes.

Unmarketable the true gift,
a tattered flower. It hides a dust of seeds.
A baby crying, a young man dying.
From this strange present,
who grows eternity?

First published in *Affirming Love*, BRF, 1999

Snowed In, Not Under

Everyone talked to strangers.
We laughed. Marvelled. Crunched.
Snow topped our boots.
Cars marooned, we remembered how to walk.
Suddenly, we had time.
Dads played in the street (with children!)
helped the house-bound.
Our neighbours gathered after dark,
straddling the road for a lamp-lit barbeque
and all the trees blossomed, white as Spring.

A Candle for Christmas

So as to shop and work and party longer
we manufacture lights to chase away
the darkest time of year.
Neighbours string coloured bulbs
on trees and window frames,
until it seems each house might be
a fairy palace, welcoming strangers
from the cold and lonely night.

Some find a welcome. Others take
their aches into the shadows.
Conscious of these, last year I saw
all lights fade beside one candle.
Had it been placed against a white wall,
under fluorescent glare,
who would have noticed,
though it burned warm, like a small sun?
But, halo-bright in that dark corner,
where finger-tip, or puff of air might
have snuffed it out,
it outlived other guiding lights,
and still shines hope into the heart.

Wait ... Follow ...

Follow the star ... the cloud ... the fire ...
high, higher, until they come to rest,
perhaps over the place where the child is.
There discover ... everything, and nothing, new.
Your quiet life unsettled, unsettling,
grow there, know ... wait ... be ...
always ready to move on.

First published in *Waiting*, SPCK, 2008

Winter Garden

Reed and branch bare
in chill winter air.

Set against the glare
of sky's alien infinity,
water's ice-cold stare –

dare, fires, to flare,
fragile-bright as birth,
or prayer.

A Christmas Carol

Come then to the stable bare
out of darkness into light,
come then to the cradle there
see the Christ-child born this night.

Mary, God has chosen thee
for the mother of His Son,
Mary, thou shalt ever be
holy mother, blessed one.

Joseph, take her for thy wife,
cherish her and call her thine.
Be a father to the life
that she carries, life divine.

In a stable born was He
mighty God held by a maid,
shepherds leave your sheep to see
lamb of God in manger laid.

Wise men, you have travelled far,
come to worship and bow down.
Guided by His shining star,
may we, too, the Saviour crown.

Come then to the stable bare
out of darkness into light,
come then to the cradle there
see the Christ-child born this night.

(Can be sung to the tune *Peacefield* or *Lyne*)

The Holly and the Ivy ~ a Sonnet

Come holly, prick and quicken me
put off feeble, faithless fear;
green of leaf and red of berry
crown of thorns, and nails, and spear.

Ivy bind me closer, tighter
to the child in manger laid,
God, the universe-creator
needing ministrations of a maid.

Hear *The Holly and the Ivy* sung
in chapel, church and shopping street;
ivy bind my faith still firmer;
holly, if I stray then meet
me, goad me back, remake me, scold me,
once again may ivy hold me.

Snow-change

Silent it came, pure, white,
changing the world outside
our window as we slept last night.
Shivering, we feel
the cold slide into danger.

Then rampant delight
shatters the calm, sullies the white.
With faces flushed the children build
a house of snow
and never care although,
should parents' wish for thaw come true,
their own hard work would melt and go.

Year of the Lord's Favour

Your birthday comes at year's dark end
to bring us hope and joy.
A thousand years, two thousand years
of Anno Domini
since those bright Christmas angels
a turning point proclaimed –
that God had come to all the world,
a Saviour who would reign.

Yet since that time how much we've lost!
The wonder and the love
You gave to us, we've thrown aside
and trampled in the mud,
for Your bright gifts at Christmas
we've swapped for glitter's toys.
Forgive us Lord, we need Your heart,
humility and voice.

So would You once again, our Lord,
be born in us today?
Cause us to care as You have done
for poor and weak and maimed.
Teach us again to worship,
pierce our complacency,
then come again in glorious power
to rule the world You made!

(Can be sung to the tune of *O Little Town of Bethlehem*)

Is my Town far from Bethlehem?

Is my town far from Bethlehem?
And can I see the stable still,
and enter in and kneel, adore?
Can I then know my Maker's will,
drive out the doubts and fears until
my all too fragile faith's made strong?

But as I worship Christ, the King
my eyes are opened and I see
that worship leads to service, love
means loving, working. Bended knee
must rise to sacrifice to Thee
my God, the living, loving Lord.

And so where age and loneliness
or clouded mind, or loss of sight
deprive your child of friendship's warmth,
give me the grace to bring the light
and joy of Christmas' merry night
to some, the lost forgotten ones.

Family Re-union

Sorry, you were saying you're exactly ... who?
Yes, I remember Great Uncle Jonathan –
moved up north – rum lot up there.
Used to see him at the Feasts –
passed away now, of course.
And so you reckon that makes you
my second cousin once removed?

No, I don't think we have met before.
Sorry to keep you standing at the door.
As you can see our house is full.
Emergency? I don't see why. You sure?
Really, we would help but we've no room at all
to put you up or even give a cup of wine.
This wretched census has brought so many
to our little town, at this time.
Any minute a baby due?
Congratulations, Joseph!
Mum-to-be is here with you!
I didn't know that you were married.
She's what? She's your betrothed? I have to say
we southern Jews would not have strayed
so far from Temple, Law or common decency.
The baby isn't yours? Oh-My-Goodness!

That's her? She's but a child!
Joseph, I'm not liking this.
Sounds like you've gone really wild –
old enough to know better, too –
a child's a big responsibility, you know.

She's crying out, 'The baby comes!'
In common decency will we succumb
and let you in? S'pose we'll have to. Come on then,
there's space downstairs where we house the beasts –
keep you both warm and dry at least,
just until the baby's born.

Who's now knocking at the door?
Dirty shepherds from the fields
been sleeping rough. They're bringing lambs,
say some angels sang to them,
made them come here!
I suspect that they've been at the beer.

We've grown quite fond of Mary and the child.
Yes, they're still here, Joseph too –
he is our cousin, after all,
it was the least that we could do.
But the other night – well, they weren't even Jews –

foreign chappies with their camels,
servants, the lot! Said they'd come to worship, here.
Not our religion – very queer –
come to worship Joseph's child.
I know he says the baby isn't his
but look at his nose, and curly hair –
just like our Simon's was. Still, I'll say this
for those Persian men, they brought gifts –
cost a lot, you can always tell.
P'raps in the end it'll work out well
for Joseph's little family. I hope they'll settle here
in Bethlehem – next door's for sale.
We'd like to see the child we rescued
grow big and strong through all our years.
Hope he brings joy to what started in tears.

Hunt the Thimble

Let me take your coat.
Have you seen our crib?
Do come and see.
We play Hunt the Thimble.
We all do, every year.
I must introduce you to Ruth.

Uncle says property,
nothing like property.
The bookshelves are always
Angela's favourite place,
on the *Concise Oxford* ...

Simon's friend Jonathan,
the father of the twins,
in the Civil Service,
secure and index-linked.
Try the mantelpiece there,
amongst the Christmas cards,
or should it be among?
Never could remember.

Gilts, my father says, gilts.
Still the thing. Stick to gilts.
Stick to them! I'd just like
to touch them in passing!
Depends what you want though.
Peace of mind. A good time.
Best for the kids. Pension.
Or something for the soul?

Or the soul for something?
Thinks. If I get a turn
I shall hide it right there,
in grandfather's turn-ups.
He's dropping off nicely.
Of course there's postage stamps,
or pictures, or gold coins.
But what about income?

Poor Ruth's daughter, Mary,
was the one who found it.
Hidden in the crib, dear.
Heaven's above! In the crib!

Time for a Baby?

Time for a baby? God, I don't think so!
First they make you sick and then they hurt – a lot.
Their birth is just the start
of taking over life in every part.
Babies make mess, need nappies changed.
They cry, they're sick and need the doc,
cause huge expense, make your whole world rock,
and, once they're grown, still cause you grief.
People say there's no relief
until your dying day.
Babies? Hey never, not for me, no way!

Time for a baby? God, I've far too much to do.
Money doesn't grow on trees.
We have to live, we have to feed!
There's my career – I mustn't miss my cue
for favour and promotion, mustn't slack or I'll lose track.

There's house to clean and meals to cook,
shopping, getting to work and back,
cards to write, presents to send –
stands to reason, at this season, I cannot spend
time on any baby
and that, I'm afraid, is that!
I know this one's poor and weak
but surely someone else can speak
up for him? I am aware that he's in danger,
but, after all, I am a stranger.

'The choice is yours,' whispers the Father of the Child,
'but know that love became this tiny stranger
so you might avoid that danger'.

Best Christmas

Why wasn't I wiping up? Was I ill?
Parents had cooked. Now replete,
presents unwrapped, thanks given,
I sat alone in the lounge,
bathed in tree-light, quiet,
while they made busy kitchen noises.
That's all I remember.
Not my age at the time.
Not the location of my brother.
Not what I'd given or received.
Only this God-full glory, this peace,
mellow, straight-transforming the room
where I'd struggled with maths,
watched silly cartoons.
This assurance I'm loved, no matter what,
safe, snuggled warm in unseen arm,
intense, unexpected, lasting mere moments.
This but once, on His birthday.

At other times,
in other places too, each one worth
its weight in gold and longer-lasting, pure,
transforming lives and not itself transformed
from baser things or simple happiness.
Hail Jesus, full of grace
at Christmas and all times.
Father, Spirit, blessed is Your coming.

Christmas Bells

Sing and ring in
rushing harmony
of clashing bells.
Tell the day
of Jesus' birth
around the town,
all up and down.

Rejoice and shout
the glorious morn
is born again.
Our world's made new
at Christmas time,
come, worship you.

The bells all sing
of new hope in
the darkest hour
their music's power
touch you with fire,
wonder inspire!

The old and new
the spoilt and true
the great and small
come, worship, all.
Born to rejoice
and to make glad
the heart of God
in this His world
and ever more.

At Christmas' Heart

Hidden, somehow, in Christmas, the poor and the wild,
those hanging from edges, the ill and defiled
and those who are searching to find their new child.

Ice-thaw

As when Christmas melts winter
in Narnia,
to you be warmth and growth and life,
bright, brave flowers, chuckling streams,
the tang of pines,
and pure, fresh mountain air.

After Christmas

Aconites

Aconites come first:
green ruffs unfold,
gild winter with sunshine.
Snowdrops purify
the short, dim days.

As You set flowers to prime our faith,
will You dig and enrich
the tired, bare earth of our lives, Lord?

Colour our bleakness
with green, white, gold;
live Your brave miracles again in us.
Christ is risen. He is risen indeed.

First published in *Leaning Towards Easter*, SPCK, 2005

Grumpy's New Year

New Year is for 'owls', extroverts, optimists –
not me, whom champagne drains,
and midnight turns to
a miserable kind of pumpkin.
Bed beckons well before twelve, any day.
But New Year firework racket
and drunken yells from even our secluded street
deprive us all of sleep
to grump on through tomorrow.

One year becomes another. So ...?
Numbers never did it for me.
And why look forward, expecting better?
We all know it might be worse.
Why link crossed, chummy-clammy hands to sing
Scots dialect none here understands
which, in translation means, I'm told:
'Should old acquaintance be forgotten

and never called to mind,
should old acquaintance be forgotten,
for the sake of old time's sake.'
Nonsense, not even a sentence, never explains
what horrors happen should this memory fail –
which scares me, as forgetting's
one thing in life at which I am improving.

As for those pesky resolutions –
quickest way I know to a guilt-trip.
See, can't even write a decent poem for New Year.
'Bah, Humbug!' I say. 'Roll on Spring!'

Song and Dance

At the ending of the year
dance a carol.
For new friends and all held dear
dance a carol.
For our days of work and leisure,
gentle sunshine, laughter, pleasure,
all the memories that we treasure,
sing a carol, dance a carol.

For the pain of birth and death
pray a love song.
Bitter wars won't stop for breath
pray a love song.
At the start of this new year,
winds of hope and frost of fear,
may we bring to God good cheer,
pray a love song, sing a love song.

A Bending of Beauty

Stooping so lowly, laying the Child
low in the manger, deep in the wild
of the hay of the manger so low,
such bending of beauty as Mary smiled.

Such weight of glory, entrusted below
to sweet Mary. How much did she know,
nourishing, cherishing Him as He grew
into our world two thousand years ago?

The priests and the soldiers and all their crew
came to hang Him high and pierce Him through.
Beautiful Mary, watching Him die,
bent with His body cradled anew.

Bearing such anguish made Mary cry,
but now they say He reigns on high.
And I'll not deny it, no not I.
I'll not deny it, no not I.

The Donkey's Song

I will bear you to Bethlehem, Mary,
the stable we find will be home for a beast.
I will rest there in Bethlehem, Mary,
and watch while you nestle your Son to your breast.

I will stand aside patiently, Mary,
while shepherds and kings come to worship your Son.
I will wait there in Bethlehem, Mary,
and nod to your lullaby, sleep in your song.

Then I'll take you to Egypt, dear Mary,
away from the hatred of Herod the king.
And your Son will grow strong there, sweet Mary,
till Herod is dead and his soldiers have gone.

Then I'll take you to Nazareth, Mary,
where your Son will work at the carpenter's bench.
There you'll watch while my son is born, Mary,
my son will carry your Son to His death.

He'll bear Him to Jerusalem, Mary.
Hosanna they'll cry, Hosanna on high.
To carry His cross through the city, Mary,
your heart will be pierced, and the donkeys will cry.

But that's not the end of the story, Mary,
for death and the grave cannot hold your Son down.
He'll up and away to glory, Mary,
and donkeys will dance, they'll dance in the dawn.

Christmas Comes

Pregnant, she could have been
stoned for adultery,
lacked the basics to give birth
when, yes, the baby came!

Crawling now, or rushing in a
jumble of emotions, whether we're
savouring the moment or wishing it over,
Christmas comes.

Our memories, sweet and bitter
vie for attention with all the
food, drink, people, presents
and children, grown.

Fleeing soon for her child's life
did she know she'd not
save him as a young man –
that Christmas comes – and goes?

And comes again, who knows?

Meeting an Angel

I would so like to meet an angel.
Not a great archangel, not Gabriel,
but just an ordinary angel, if there is
such a thing as an ordinary angel.

Afterwards people would say,
'What was he like, and how was he dressed?'
and I would not remember things like that.
Only remember that I was so blessed.
I would remember the joy in his face,
the music in his voice when he spoke my name.
For the first time know the meaning of Grace,
and that life would never be the same
again, never the same again.

Twelfth Night

Someone said it doesn't matter
if you leave the decorations up
till after Twelfth Night. Doesn't matter!!
Don't you know how bitter is the cup
of woes and terrors that befall
a housewife who ignores the rule
that every twig of greenery, every shiny ball
and star, the tree, the tinsel, Yule
Log with imitation snow, the holly
and the ivy and the fairy lights
must all be put away before
the end of those twelve Christmas nights?

And what will happen if you don't?
Seven years bad luck or is it ten?
For starters your hair falls out, and then your teeth,
your boiler bursts and those smiling men
who should turn up to fix it
say their van broke down
and catch you next day in your dressing gown ...

Your saucepans stick
your children are sick
the car won't start
'cos the battery's flat
and the dear little goldfish
eats the cat.
I don't believe it – it don't seem right
but still – I'll take mine down tonight.

Acrostic for Epiphany

Emptied of bright decorations, house and life loom bare.

Promise of Spring, of Easter, through dark chill seems so very far.

I wonder: long ago, those occult foreigners, did they return

Puzzled and puzzling to their own land; their own stars?

Having met the child, his parents, Herod, heard tell of virgin birth and

Angel choirs, their brief epiphany affected them – how?

Now, too, has Christmas changed the world for you and me in this new

Year – like a painful birth brought change and hope – or danger, fear ...?

EPIPHANY says, 'Fear not but know, near or far off, you are most dear.'

Joseph's Story

You see, it was not given to me to understand.
Mary understood more, much more,
well, you know – mothers and sons.
Women have a closeness to their children
that we men can never know.
But remember, the angel did speak to me,
ah, yes, he spoke to me all right.
And that's something you never forget.

The journey to Bethlehem was hard;
then finding no room at the inn,
and having to make do in that stable,
that was harder – what a night.
But the birth was easy, thank God,
as easy as any birth can be, that is.

Hardest of all, though, was being told
we had to up and clear off to Egypt.
That was an angel again, you see, who told us.
Mary still weak from her labour,
a new-born baby, not much money left.
Those gifts from the wise men
came in useful, all right. Especially the gold.
They weren't just fancy, pretty presents you know.
Kept us going till we were settled in a new home.

We still had a little of the gold left
when we came back, back to Nazareth, that is.
Enough to get me started in the carpentry business.
Mind you it took those northerners a while to accept me,
being a southerner myself. A bit suspicious, they are.
But once they do get to know you they're all right.

He's making a good carpenter, young Jesus,
strong hands and a good eye,
a feeling for the grain in the wood.
And not afraid of hard work.
But I can't forget what happened
when we went up to Jerusalem for the feast.
Found Him in the temple, we did;
twelve years old and holding His own
with those long-beards, discussing the Law.

Don't think He'll stay with me much longer.
He'll be off. Doing His own thing.
No. Not His own thing.
He talked about doing His Father's business.
And I'm telling you, He didn't mean me and
   carpentry!

Index